Mindfulness is being calm.

Mindfulness is being in the present moment.

Mindfulness is being peaceful.

Mindfulness is being supernatural.

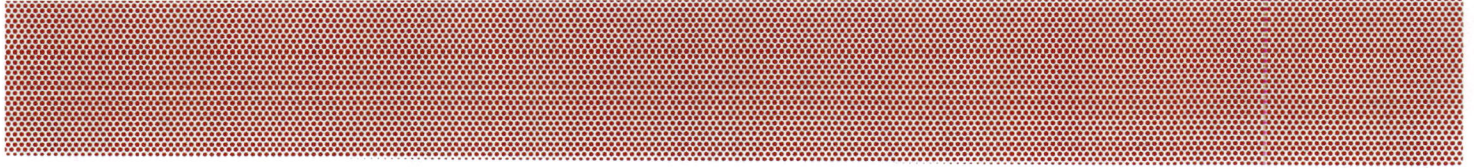

Mindfulness is clearing clutter from our mind.

Mindfulness is emptying the mind.

Mindfulness is focusing on your senses.

Mindfulness is going inward.

Mindfulness is relaxing each muscle in your body.

**Mindfulness is relaxing
your mind.**

Mindfulness is
sitting in silence.

Mindfulness is smiling.

Mindfulness is spending time with nature.

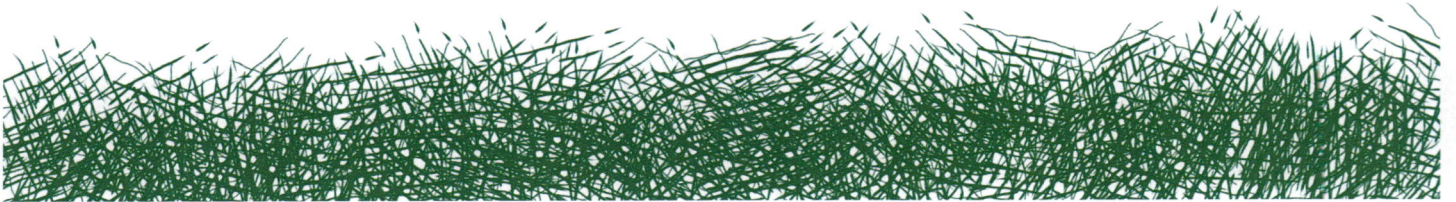

Mindfulness is spending time
with yourself.

Mindfulness is to be with your breath.

Activity :- Turn on gentle music and find a comfortable seated position, either on the floor with crossed legs or in a chair. Then, take a few deep breaths and clear your mind, focusing solely on the sensation of your inhales and exhales. Simply sit in silence and be present in the moment.